# The CASPARS

Clinical Tools for Assessing Client Risks & Strengths:

- Emotional Expressiveness
- Family Relationships
- Peer Relationships
- Sexuality
- Family Embeddedness in Community

## PROFESSIONAL MANUAL

Jane F. Gilgun, Ph.D, LICSW

Jane F. Gilgun, Ph.D., LICSW, is a professor, School of Social Work, University of Minnesota, Twin Cities, 1404 Gortner Avenue, St. Paul, MN 55108 USA. E-mail: jgilgun@umn.edu. Professor Gilgun publishes widely in academic journals. Her books, children's books, and articles are available on Amazon and for Kindle, iPad, Nook, & other e-readers.

# ALSO BY JANE GILGUN

## Children's Books

*Busjacked!*
*Emma and her Forever Person*
*Five Little Cygnets Cross the Bundoran Road*
*Patrick and the Magic Mountain*
*The King's Toast*
*The Little Pig Who Didn't go to Market*
*The Picking Flower Garden*
*Turtle Night at Playa Grande*
*Will the Soccer Star*

## Books

*Child Sexual Abuse: From Harsh Realities to Hope*
*Children with Serious Conduct Issues*
*I Want to Show You: Poems*
*The NEATS: A Child & Family Assessment*
*Thorns Have Roses: A Story of Family Recovery from Clergy Sexual Abuse*

## Manuals

*Lemons or Lemonade? An Anger Workbook for Kids*
*Lemons or Lemonade? A Manual for Professionals and Parents of Kids*
*Lemons or Lemonade? An Anger Workbook for Teens*
*Lemons or Lemonade? A Manual for Professionals and Parents of Teens*
*Readiness to Adopt Children with Special Needs*

Jane Gilgun is a professor and writer. She has many articles and assessment tool available on social media websites such as scribd.com, Amazon Kindle, and smashwords.com.

# Getting Started with the CASPARS

**The CASPARS** are a set of five clinical rating scales for work with children ages 6 to 12 and their families. They are emotional expressiveness, family relationships, peer relationships, sexual, and family embeddedness in the community. CASPARS is an acronym that stands for Clinical Assessment Package for Client Risks and Strengths.

The tools are based on ecological, strengths-based practice, case study and survey research on persons who have overcome risks for adverse outcomes, research on risk and resilience, attachment theory, and clinical experience.

They are meant to help in assessment, treatment planning, to monitor the course of treatment, and to provide outcome scores. They also have the potential to guide conversations that can lead both children and social service professionals to new understandings.

The CASPARS are most useful to professionals and agencies whose practice is based on principles that fit with the ideas on which the CASPARS are based.

## Principles on Which the CASPARS are Based

Within the last decade, the demands of managed health care and evidence-based approaches have put heavy pressure on service providers. Not only are practitioners enjoined to use best research evidence, but they must do their work in as short a time as possible to hold down costs. At the same time, they must demonstrate the effectiveness of their interventions, preferably with quantified outcomes (Gilgun, 2005; Gray, 2002; Sackett et al, 2000). Demands for efficiency, efficacy, cost containment, and best research evidence are part of the context in which contemporary clinical practice takes place.

Another recent development is the understanding of the importance of identifying and building upon client strengths in order to foster clients' capacities for dealing with their risks (Fraser, 1997; Gilgun, 2004a, b, & c, 2002; 1996a & b; Saleebey, 2002; Smith & Carlson, 1997; van Eys & Dodge,1999). Solution-focused therapy, narrative therapy, and competency-based practices are examples of this trend. Many of these approaches are also brief treatments that focus on capacity-building. Developmental psychopathology, a branch of developmental psychology that studies high risks

groups in order to identify factors that lead to positive and negative outcomes, provides many useful concepts to therapists interested in identifying and building on client capacities (Gilgun, 1996b; Gilgun et al, 1999; Gilgun, Klein, & Pranis, 2000; van Eys & Dodge, 1999).

The clinical assessment tools that I've developed over the past several years are designed to respond to the contemporary demands that clinicians experience. They are based on best research evidence and give equal consideration to client strengths and deficits. They guide clinicians to focus on aspects of client functioning that research and theory have identified as fundamental to emotional and psychological wellbeing.

These instruments potentially can contribute to efficiency in assessment and treatment planning and thus reduce time clients spend in treatment. In addition, the tools were developed for practice with children and families where the children have experienced trauma and other adversities and have developed behaviors that bring them to the attention of clinical practitioners.

The behaviors include conduct disorders, self-harming behaviors, and inappropriate sexual behaviors. The assessment tools are short, easy to use, can be scored so as to give quantified outcomes, and are based on research evidence and clinical expertise. The tools that I've developed are:

• the Clinical Assessment Package for Client Risks and Strengths (CASPARS), tested on children and their families where the children are ages 5 to 13. These tools are the subject of the present manual. The manual and the tools are available at

• the 4-D, strengths-based tools for youth in out-of-home care, tested on youth ages 12 to 19 and their families, available at http://www.scribd.com/doc/26474371/The-4-D-a-Strengths-Based-Assessment-for-Children-in-Out-of-Home-Care; and

• Risk Assessment in Child Welfare, useful to public child welfare practice and untested. The 4-D and the child welfare tools are available at http://www.scribd.com/doc/20370958/A-Guided-Tour-of-Risk-Assessment-in-Child-Welfare/. This manual focuses on the CASPARS.

These tools were constructed according to the tenets of evidence-based practice, which has developed from evidence-based medicine (EBM). EBM is composed of three dimensions: best research evidence, clinical expertise, and patients' wants and preferences. Proponents of EBM state that practice has several components, including diagnosis, treatment, and outcome. Each of these phases of practice requires the application of best research evidence (Evidence-Based Medicine Working Group, 1992; Gilgun, 2005; Sackett et al, 2000; Straus & McAlister, 2000). These components of medical practice are similar to the practice of psychotherapy.

The CASPARS, the 4-D, and the child welfare tools are not only based on best research evidence, but they incorporate the professional experiences of clinical psychologists and social workers. In addition, the CASPARS and the 4-D have been piloted so as to see how clients respond to the concepts that the instruments incorporate. They are designed to help in assessment and treatment planning, to monitor the course of treatment, and to provide outcome scores. Thus, the tools are consistent with major tenets of evidence-based practice.

Psychometric testing has been performed on the five tools that compose the CASPARS. Details on the 4-D are in Gilgun (2002, 2004c and on scribd.com/professorjane). The strengths-based child welfare tools are untested. The coefficient alphas for the CASPARS and the 4-D are .9 and above. Nunnnaly (1978) stated that alphas of .9 are required for instruments that are meant to be used with individuals. These nine instruments have reached this high standard. In addition, the CASPARS instruments have high inter-rater reliabilities and good construct validity (Gilgun, 1999a).

The purpose of this manual is to demonstrate the features of one set of strengths-based tools—the CASPARS—and, in doing this, to provide a model for the development of other strengths-based instruments that could be customized to a variety of settings, populations, and theoretical frameworks. Clinical practitioners could use some of the ideas in this chapter and develop their own instruments. If there are items in the instruments that might be useful, then clinicians are encouraged to use them, with attribution, and to add them to their own custom-fit tools. Taynor, Nelson, and Daugherty (1990) provide another account of how practitioners worked with a University-based researcher to develop and test family assessment and outcome measures.

The 4-D for youth in out-of-home care is an example of how the ideas of the CASPARS can be used in the construction of other instruments. The conceptual base of the 4-D is the Circle of Courage, an American Indian Medicine Wheel that incorporates contemporary theories of human development (Brendtro, Brokenleg, & van Brocken, 1999; Gilgun, 2002, 2004c). This is not the conceptual base of the CASPARS, although the CASPARS are based on some of the same theories as the Circle of Courage. In addition, the 4-D are structured similarly to the CASPARS in that they give equal consideration to client strengths and risks and provide two scores: a risk score and a strengths score. Like the CASPARS, the 4-D are intended to be useful for assessment, intervention planning, predicting outcome of interventions, and the evaluation of the effects of treatment.

Guidelines for choosing assessment and evaluation tools are available at http://www.scribd.com/doc/23611989/Choosing-Assessment-and-Evaluation-Tools-for-Direct-Practice/. A paper describing the CASPARS and the 4-D is available at http://www.scribd.com/doc/38584515/A-Strengths-Based-Approach-to-Child-Family-Assessment/.

**The CASPARS**

The CASPARS are based on research and theory from developmental psychopathology, in-depth case study interviews, and the practice experience of social work clinicians and clinical psychologists. The five instruments composing the CASPARS are: (a) Emotional Expressiveness, (b) Family Relationships, (c) Family's Embeddedness in the Community, (d) Peer Relationships, and (e) Sexuality.

As clinical rating scales (scales that are to be filled out by practitioners and not by clients), the instruments are designed to fit and add to practice. The instruments tap into risks and strengths that reside in individuals, families, peer groups, and community. The measurement of individual functioning alone would neglect the multiple ecologies with which individuals interact (Beck, 1997; van Eys & Dodge, 1999). The CASPARS were tested for practice in such settings as child mental health and child welfare, including foster care, in-home services, and residential treatment.

The CASPARS instruments are composed of concrete indicators of assets and risks. The items were developed through 11 years of in-depth case study research conducted with adults who had experienced a range of childhood and adolescent risks. In the course of conducting case studies, it became clear that a variety of pathways lead to multiple developmental outcomes, some of which were quite adaptive and others maladaptive (Gilgun, 2000).

The factors that consistently differentiated good and poor outcomes were grouped under the domains that the present instruments represent: family relationships, emotional expressiveness, sexuality, peer relationships, and family's embeddedness in the community (Gilgun, 2002, 2004a & c; 1999a, 1999b, 1996a, 1996b, 1992, 1991, 1990; Gilgun et al, 2000; Gilgun et al, 1999).

The identification and conceptualization of the domains and the development of items were facilitated by research and theory on developmental psychopathology (Gilgun, 1996a & b; Masten & Wright, 1998; Mahoney & Bergman, 2002; van Eys & Dodge, 1999; Werner & Smith, 1992) and social work's ecological, strengths-based perspectives (Baker & Steiner, 1995; DeJong & Miller, 1996; Goldstein, 1990; Greene, Jensen, & Jones, 1996; Saleebey, 2002; Tracy et al, 1994).

Other related research provided added direction for the development of the CASPARS instruments, such as research in child development that recognizes appropriate emotional expressiveness as linked to academic and social success and good mental health across the life span, from childhood to old age (Boyum & Parke, 1995; Cassidy & Asher, 1992; Halberstadt, Cassidy et al, 1995; Parke & Ladd, 1992; Parker & Asher, 1987; Roberts & Strayer, 1996).

Finally, the practice knowledge of social work clinicians and clinical psychologists with long-term experience with children who had experienced adversities and their families contributed to the instruments' development. These clinicians critiqued drafts of the instruments, suggested additions and deletions, and participated in the piloting.

*Key Concepts*

The CASPARS instruments, as well as the other strengths-based measures, are built around several key concepts, including risks, assets, emotional expressiveness, family relationships, family embeddedness in the community, and peer relationships.

*Risks.* A probabilistic concept, risks predict that a portion of an at-risk group will have an associated outcome, but they cannot predict that any one individual will have the outcome (Masten, 1994; Masten et al, 1991; Rutter, 1987). Examples of risks include family separations and losses, a history of childhood and adolescent maltreatment, unsafe neighborhoods, family isolation, structurally-based disadvantage and discrimination, exposure to persons who model violent behaviors, inability to access internal states such as emotions and wants, and genetic risks predisposing individuals to particular types of physiological reactivity (Cicchetti, 1987; Rende & Plomin, 1993; Richters & Martinez, 1993; Werner & Smith, 1992).

*Assets.* Assets too, can be considered probabilistic concepts and are factors associated with adaptive outcomes. They predict that a proportion of groups with assets will have good outcomes, but they are not deterministic on the individual level. Some persons with assets have unsatisfactory outcomes and behaviors because they are not able to use whatever assets they have to moderate risks, or because the risks overwhelm assets (Masten, 1994; Masten et al, 1991; Rutter, 1987). Assets include factors such as high IQ, physical attractiveness, verbal facility, caring parents, safe neighborhoods, adequate family income, and well-functioning schools (Cicchetti, 1987; Garmezy & Masten, 1994; Masten et al, 1991; Richters & Martinez, 1993; Rutter, 1987; Werner & Smith, 1992). Assets become protective factors when they can be shown to have facilitated the overcoming of risks (Gilgun, 1996a; Masten, 1994).

*Emotional expressiveness.* When at-risk individuals have opportunities to express their emotions in constructive ways—both positive and painful emotional experiences—they are at lowered risk for adverse outcomes (Erickson, Korfmacher, & Egeland, 1992; Fraiberg, Adelson, & Shapiro, 1975). Conversely, at-risk persons who distance themselves from their emotions and do not experience or express them are at high risk for developing adverse outcomes (Cicchetti et al, 1993; Garmezy & Masten, 1994; Gilgun, 2002, 1999b, 1996a, 1996b, 1991, 1990; Masten, 1994; Rutter, 1987; Werner & Smith, 1992).

Emotional expressiveness is embedded in a web of positive human relationships within and outside families (Boyum & Parke, 1995; Gilgun, 1996b; Cassidy et al, 1995; Roberts & Strayer, 1996).

Among the benefits of emotional expressiveness is its facilitation of the sorting through of conflicting thoughts, feelings, and values and a consequent cognitive restructuring that can include many new understandings, including (a) the reduction of the sense of self as defective, (b) a renewed sense of the self as connected to other persons, and (c) an affirmation of positive goals and values.

***Family relationships.*** Consistent with attachment research and research on risk, assets, and protective factors, emotional expressiveness probably develops from secure attachments to parents and/or parental figures during infancy, early childhood, and across the life span (Bowlby, 1973; Cicchetti, 1987; Egeland et al, 1993; Masten & Garmezy, 1985). Emotional expressiveness is associated with long-term positive relationships with others.

Individuals who have a capacity for emotional expressiveness grow up in circumstances that afford them some assets, such as parental figures who maintain harmonious relationships with each other, family members who show sensitivity to children's feelings and wants, and family members who recognize the children's accomplishments. Positive adaptation is problematic if individuals experienced disharmony, insensitivity, and maltreatment within families of origin.

***Family embeddedness in the community.*** Families who are positively connected to extended family members and to other persons in the wider community have access to material and emotional resources. Such access bodes well for the adequacy of family functioning (Gilgun, in press, 1999b; 1996b; Werner & Smith, 1992). Involvement in community activities, work that is meaningful, and the availability of safe playgrounds, libraries and other community-based resources are some of the characteristics of families who are embedded in their communities. The converse is resource-poor communities and disconnection from persons and institutions that might offer emotional and material support.

***Peer relationships.*** Positive family relationships and a capacity for emotional expressiveness also are correlated with positive relationships with peers (Boyum & Parke, 1995; Gilgun, 1996b; Cassidy et al, 1995; Roberts & Strayer, 1996). Assets related to peer groups are friendships that endure over time, friends who behave in pro-social ways and who do well in school, friends who express a range of emotions and who respect the feelings of others, and the capacity to feel part of a peer group. Persons with problematic outcomes have relationships with peers who feel alienated from school and most other persons, who perform anti-social acts, and who inhibit their own expression of painful and private feelings and denigrate those of others.

***Sexuality.*** Individuals whose sexual development and behaviors are adequate have exposure to healthy sexual attitudes and appropriate information about sexuality whether in families of origin or elsewhere. They experience sexuality as a natural part of being human. If they had experienced sexual abuse, they had opportunities to cope with and/or overcome the effects of the abuse. Persons who exhibit problematic sexual behaviors rarely had such positive experiences. Risks for poor sexual functioning include a history of child sexual abuse, exposure to distorted and partial information about sexuality, exposure to sexual boundary violations, and lack of opportunity to discuss sexual maltreatment and to obtain accurate information about sexuality (Gil & Johnson, 1993; Gilgun, 1996a, 1996b; Friedrich, Grambsch et al, 1992; Salter, 1988). Children, adolescents, and adults who have a history of sexual abuse and/or a history of exposure to distorted, sexist attitudes toward sexuality and have not experienced moderators of such experiences are at risk to develop sexual issues of various sorts.

## Piloting

The five CASPARS instruments were developed on the basis of the above research and theory. Reliability and validity studies were conducted with a sample of 146 girls and boys and their biological and foster families. (See Gilgun, 1999a, for details on sampling, testing, reliability and validity.) The children had a variety of therapeutic issues, neuropsychological conditions, and behavioral difficulties, as well as several types of maltreatment, including physical abuse (38%), psychological maltreatment (41%), sexual abuse (58%), and witnessing physical and/or sexual abuse (47%). More than half the sample had been in out-home care at least once in their lives. A large portion had been in therapeutic foster homes and in individual, group, and family therapy. Professionals such as social workers, child care workers, therapeutic foster parents, and psychologists filled out the instruments on the children.

## Description of the CASPARS

As clinical rating scales; the CASPARS are designed to guide practitioners to identify and work with strengths and deficits in children and families where the children have a range of adjustment issues. The overall goal of treatment is to increase strengths and reduce deficits. Number of items range from 13 to 20. Table 1 describes the instruments and their coefficient alphas and inter-rater reliabilities.

### Clinical Rating Scales

As clinical rating scales, that is, scales that are filled out by practitioners and not by clients, the instruments are designed to fit and add to practice. The instruments direct practitioners' attention to risks and strengths that reside in individuals, families, peer groups, and community.

Each of the tools is composed of items that have a risk side and a strength side. Figure 1 shows the first two items of the emotional expressiveness instrument.

The items are purposely broad in scope in order to help practitioners organize the information they already have of clients and their situations.

Thus, scoring requires clinical judgment. Clinicians draw upon their multiple sources of knowledge, such as direct contact with children and their biological and foster families, contact with collaterals such as teachers, social workers, and medical practitioners, and record reviews.

### Scoring

Scoring is a two-step process based on knowledge of children gained from sources just discussed. First, practitioners decide if children has a strength, a risk, or an inconsistency on an item. Then they circle the number that most closely fits their assessment of the children's status on that item. Inconsistency means the children sometimes shows the quality and sometimes does not.

The instruments provide two scores: a strengths score and a risk score that are calculated by adding the scores of each column.

### Reliability and Validity

The CASPARS have reached the "gold standard" of a coefficient alpha of .9 and the inter-rater reliabilities are in the showing high reliability. The indicators of validity are highly satisfactory

---

**Figure 1: The First Two Items of Emotional Expressiveness**

**Scoring**

3=high strength
2=medium strength
1=low strength

3=high risk
2=medium risk
1=low risk

| Strengths | | | | Risks | |
|---|---|---|---|---|---|

1. Children feels connected to at least one other prosocial person.

   3          2          1          0          2          3

2. When stressed, children seeks a person, a setting, or an activity that provides a safe have.

   3          2          1          0          2          3

---

### Missing Information

Sometimes practitioners don't have the information they need to complete the CASPARS. When this happens, practitioners can leave the items blank. They can obtain the information later.

If practitioners must have a score for an item, but they don't have the information, score both sides of the item as a mixed; that is, give a score of 1 for both the strength and the risk. If the practitioner obtains information later, then the items can be rescored to reflect the new information.

### Scoring the Items

Responding to the items is a two-step process. First. practitioners decide if the appropriate response is yes, no, or mixed. Decisions are based upon evidence; that is, specific instances that show that children has a particular quality, shows particular behaviors, and has particular supports from adults and peers in the various environments in which children live their lives. "Yes" represents a strength and "no" represents a risk. Mixed means there is inconsistency, where the children sometimes shows that quality and sometimes does not.

The next step is to decide how much of strength or how much of a risk the children has. The range is from 1 to 5 for both risks and strengths. Figure 2 shows the rating scale of the CASPARS.

| Figure 2: Scoring the CASPARS | |
| --- | --- |
| **Strength** | **Risk** |
| 3=high strength | 3=high risk |
| 2=medium strength | 2=medium risk |
| 1=low strength | 1=low risk |
| 0=don't know/doesn't apply | |

As practitioners decide upon which score to give, we encourage them to think of *a child who is functioning at an optimal level.* A standard could be what practitioners would expect from their own children. Children who are functioning optimally are doing well in school, getting along at home, are appropriately emotionally expressive, well-adjusted sexually, behaving in pro-social ways, have strong emotional connections to families and friends, have long-term relationships with peers and adults that foster the sharing of personal and private information and that model and reward pro-social behaviors. These children would be contributing to the well-being of others through being helpful to others; community service activities also are an important part of giving to others. In addition, children are optimistic about the future and are making realistic plans for the future.

Other indicators of optimal functioning includes doing well when others behave unfairly, as when a children who is dealing with adversity is not treated with understanding and sensitivity.

The optimally functioning children recognizes the inappropriate behaviors of others and/or seeks help in coping with such inappropriate behaviors. In other words, the children respond appropriately to inappropriate behaviors.

*Two scores*. The instruments yield two scores: a risk score and an asset score. Two scores often puzzle practitioners who are accustomed to instruments that provide only one. Since the goal of treatment is to increase assets and decrease risks, both assets and risks need to be identified and their relative strengths assessed. Furthermore, conceptually, risks and assets are not the same. The idea of two scores builds upon the assumption that persons can have positive and negative aspects of a single broad attribute. Others have noted this. As Erikson (1950/1963) demonstrated in his theory of psychosocial development, the notion of nuclear conflict posits that aspects of the same quality co-exist within persons, such as capacities for trust and mistrust. In addition, semantic differentials are composed of bi-polar items, although these instruments provide one score.

With two scores, children can be classified according to their mix of strengths and risks as shown in Figure 3 below. The ideal is to move children into a high strengths/low risk classification. Two scores helps clinicians and clients identify and work with both strengths and risks. This classification can help with triage; that is to help make decisions about the appropriate types and duration of treatment. Types and length of treatment can be guided by the classification.

## Figure 3: Classification by Strengths and Risks

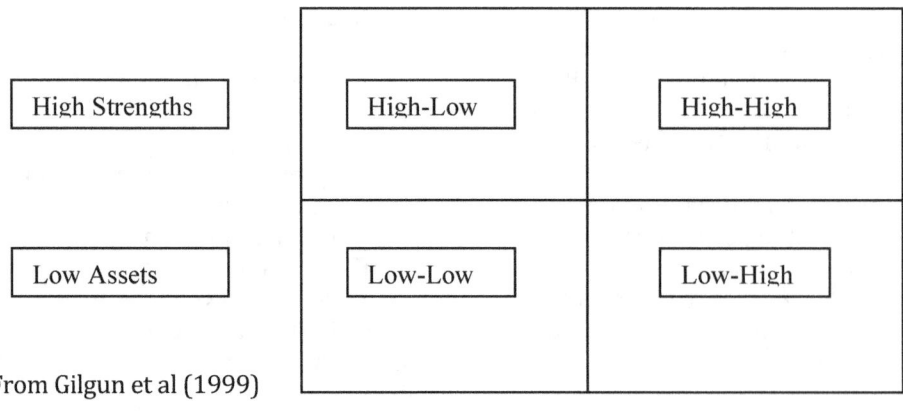

From Gilgun et al (1999)

Scores can also be graphed. Most children begin treatment high in risks and low in assets, at least on the issues that brought them into treatment in the first place. As discussed, the goal of treatment is to reduce risks and increase assets. Figure 3 below shows the graph of a successful course of treatment when clients began as low-high and ended as high-low. In those cases, the asset line intersects with the risks line.

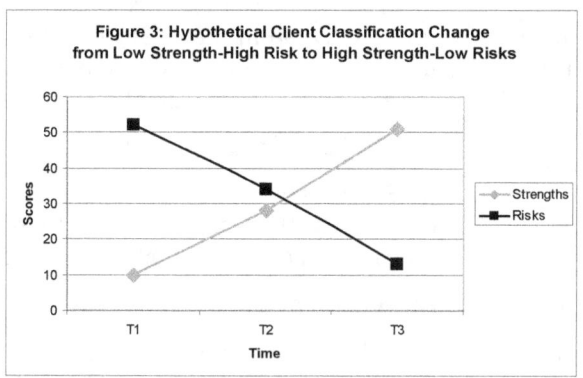

Using graphs to assess the effects of treatment has many benefits. They are a visual representation of progress or lack of progress in treatment. Clients can see for themselves how they are responding to treatment. Such easy to interpret information can spark discussions and insights about what is working and not working in treatment in a variety of settings. That is, clinicians can talk to clients directly about their progress and can discuss the case in group and peer supervision. Finally, having scores and graphs documents the effectiveness of treatment. Such documentation is important to funders and to the general public, as well as to clinicians, clients, and their agencies.

## The Psychometrics of the CASPARS

The CASPARS have excellent psychometric properties, with coefficient alphas of .9 or above, the "gold" standard for instruments meant to be used with individuals Nunnally, 1978; Rosenthal, 1994). There is much less room for unreliable and inconsistent tools when individuals are being evaluated. In group evaluations, the errors of instruments tend to average out. Psychological and educational tools often are group measurements and thus have lower standards of reliability.

Coefficient alpha is the most important test of the reliability of an instrument because they show whether the items of the instrument are measuring the same thing and not a hodgepodge of unrelated phenomena. They should be the first test of reliability, even if other measures of reliability also will be used (DeVellis, 1991; Nunnally, 1978). If the coefficient alpha is low, with low being .40 or lower, then the instrument should be reconstructed. It

simply will not reliably tell anything about what is being measured.

Table 1 shows the coefficient alphas of the CASPARS.

Table 1 Coefficient Alphas for the CASPARS

| No. of Items | Instrument | Alphas |
| --- | --- | --- |
| 14 | Emo. Exp.g | .94 |
| 20 | Fam. Rel. | .97 |
| 13 | Embed. | .96 |
| 16 | Peer. Rel. | .90 |
| 13 | Sexuality | .90 |

## Item Total Analysis

The item-total analysis of CASPARS instruments was well within the acceptable range. The lowest individual item-total correlation was .54; almost all the correlations were in the .70 and .80 range, with means varying from .63 to .80. (See Table 1.) In the construction of achievement tests and tests of ability, item-total correlations from 0 to .40 are expected. Items that are kept have the highest correlations with the total score, although when theory supports such items for inclusion, Nunnally (1978) recommends that the items be maintained.

In constructing clinical instruments, which have fewer items than achievement and ability tests and which are designed to be used with individuals, more stringent criteria are required. Item-total correlations of .50 or .60 might be more appropriate for clinical tools. The CASPARS instruments meet these standards.

Item-total analysis is a form of testing for internal consistency and indirectly demonstrates content validity (Nunnally, 1978). This analysis provides additional support for the content validity as well as the reliability of the CASPARS instruments.

## Content Validity

The CASPARS appear to have adequate content validity, as we drew upon multiple sources of information, including the Circle of Courage, research and theory on risk and resilience, social work's strengths perspective, the CASPARS instruments (Gilgun, 1999, Gilgun et al, 1999) and practitioner experience.

## Face Validity

Experienced social workers and one clinical psychologist were deeply involved in the development of the tools. They provided rigorous critique of the CASPARS and suggested the elimination of some items and the addition of others. The instrumented was also piloted providing further opportunities to ensure that the tools contained items relevant to practice.

## The Field Test:
## Conversations with Users

Conversations with users of the CASPARS provide helpful information on how to use them.

### CASPARS as Helpful

Many professionals who used the CASPARS in the field test found that the tools helped them to get to know children better and brought important new information to light. The CASPARS served as guides to conversations, often when professionals were doing other things with children, such as driving them long distances. In the course of talking about the topics the CASPARS suggest, children sometimes opened up in ways they have not done before. Some children did not want to talk to practitioners. In those cases, practitioners completed the CASPARS based on the multiple other sources of information they had. Those who were most satisfied with the tool talked both to the children and to the multiple others who are resources to children.

The CASPARS helped in treatment planning. A social worker said, "The CASPARS led to some wonderful conversations with children and helped me think and do more about preparing kids for independent living." Another user reported that completing the CASPARS helped him to stop and re-evaluate what he was doing with his kids. He found things he'd been overlooking through using the CASPARS. Another practitioner said the CASPARS not only gave her some new ideas about her work with children but they also gave care providers more direction.

A practitioner who ran an independent living program for teenagers used some of the items of the CASPARS for discussion questions for group work with teens ages 17-19 and who had been meeting for several months. They used the CASPARS to interview each other. This practitioner found to questions to be "real good icebreakers" and said he learned a lot about the teens that he said he might not otherwise have known. He said about the CASPARS, "Thumbs up."

A few social workers reported that they used the CASPARS to test their ideas about children. For example, a children who might have issues with attachment might not see the value of confiding in others or having others confide in them, which are topics covered in the CASPARS. These questions can help practitioners get a better understanding of the level of trust and distrust that children have.

### Limited Direct Contact with Children

Some users reported that they had limited direct contact with children. In these cases, their information came from multiple other sources.

### Fit With Practice

For many practitioners, the CASPARS fit with and add to their practice, as the above discussion demonstrates. Several social workers said that the CASPARS would be really effective for intensive work, such as psychotherapy, where therapists see kids once a week, observe their behaviors in school, and keep in weekly touch with teachers and care providers. One social worker in therapeutic foster care said, "If we did our own therapy that would be a great way to use CASPARS." She said that they also could be helpful in team approaches to work with children, where therapists and care providers could use them. For her, the CASPARS had many things professionals could talk to children about. "This is one of the better ones I've seen as far as questions go," she said. She added that she does not see children often enough to be able to use the CASPARS effectively.

Where there were difficulties fitting the CASPARS to practice, social workers saw their practice as supporting the work with others, not having much direct contact with children, and dealing either with on-going crises or with basic issues such as personal hygiene.

Such concerns could be training issues, at least partially. The for agency-level goals that they CASPARS help develop do not preclude individualized goals for particular cases. Furthermore, individualized goals are likely to fit within the broad scope of the concepts of the CASPARS.

### Subjectivity of the CASPARS

Several service providers expressed concern about the "subjectivity" involved in evaluating information about children and the services they receive and in deciding upon a score. Such subjectivity can be reduced to some degree by on-going training on the use of the CASPARS and on the meanings of the concepts on which they are based.

On the other hand, some subjectivity appears to be inherent in clinical tools. The very nature of being human suggests that even when two practitioners are confronted with identical information delivered in identical formats, they may still not reach the same conclusions. The best the CASPARS can do is to help practitioners organize a great deal of information and to lead them to use this information in their work with children.

### Intrusiveness of Sexuality Items

Some practitioners observed that the CASPARS ask good questions and they are not invasive. On the other hand, intrusiveness was an issue for some social workers. They cited in particular the sexuality items of the mastery (knowing) instrument. Although some social workers expressed comfort in talking about sexuality with children, other did not get into sensitive areas with children unless there is a problem about that area. Still others felt unprepared to deal with children's sexuality. Some noted that children don't want to talk about it anyway. Those who struggled with the sexuality items stated it was up to children's therapist to deal with sexuality.

Agencies will have to make decisions about whether their practitioners talk about sexuality with children. If they want this, then they must also provide training on why it's important and how to talk to children about sexuality.

### Issues and Challenges in Assessing Children

Several practitioners pointed out the challenges inherent in using clinical instruments with children and getting accurate pictures of children. The children can change from day to day, week to week. Some children simply do not want to talk about themselves out of fear, mistrust, or "therapy fatigue." Some may simply have not learned how to reach deep into themselves in order to understand their past and present  This too is a training issue that agencies will confront when they use the CASPARS.

### Issues Inherent in Assessing Roles of Others

Several social workers expressed difficulties in responding to the roles of others items. In some cases, they wondered if other professionals' assessments were influenced by their own concerns about being judged and their desires to show that they are effective.    Thus, sometimes other professionals rated children higher than the practitioners thought warranted. Other times, they thought other professionals rated children lower so as to be able to maintain the children in the placement and in the other settings where children was getting services.

This, too, is an training issue that agencies will confront if they choose to use the CASPARS.

### Implementation Issues

Through interviews with practitioners, we also found that implementation is a major issue. This showed itself in different ways: the amount of training that may be necessary for best use of the CASPARS, the sheer amount of paperwork that many practitioners must complete, and the duplication of the CASPARS with other required paperwork. Further details are in Gilgun and Chalmers (2002). This are serious issues that could threaten the usefulness of the CASPARS. Adn

As stated earlier, the ideas on which the CASPARS are based require considerable study. One of the main reasons the first author wrote the paper on the integrative framework on which the CASPARS is based (Gilgun, 2002) was to teach herself how the ideas fit together as possible assessment tools.

As practitioners used the CASPARS, some became more adept and they were pleased with the helpfulness of the CASPARS.

### Concerns About Strengths-Based Instruments

Conversations with users surfaced some concerns about using strengths-based instruments. Several social workers voiced the concern that many funders only are interested in client risks and would wonder why services are needed at all if clients have strengths.

Though this issue can only be explored through conversations with funders, which is beyond the scope of the present research. On the more hopeful side, one agency administrator said that, on the contrary, the funders of his agency want practitioners to track both whether the services are promoting strengths and decreasing risks. Concerns that funders may require children to be moved to a less expensive setting if they do well was a major issue for some social workers. This requires serious discussion with funders.

### Future Work with the CASPARS

Future work with the CASPARS themselves involves evaluating their inter-rater reliabilities and doing construct validity studies and predictive validity studies. Inter-rater reliabilities depend upon a group of practitioners having a common framework for assessment, intervention, and evaluation.

In order to do them, the practitioners who participate must undergo training on the ideas of the CASPARS.

For the field study, we chose to concentrate on encouraging practitioners to use the CASPARS and to leave the inter-rater reliability testing to another time.

Construct validity studies test how well instruments correlate with other instruments thought to measure the same thing and whether they do not correlate with instruments thought not to measure the same thing. We did not do construct validity studies because of our concerns with the amount of paperwork that practitioners were already required to do.

Finally, having a sense of the predictive validity of the CASPARS would increase confidence in them. The predicted outcome could be something quite simple, such as whether reach their individualized goals once they are ready to move to another setting.

## SUMMARY

The CASPARS is a set of clinical rating scales tested on children ages 12 to 19 and who have experienced adversities in childhood and adolescence. The tools of the CASPARS are emotional expressiveness, family relationships, family embeddedness in the community, peer relationships, and sexuality. Designed to respond to the standards of practice that have become prominent during the past decade or so, they give equal consideration to client strengths and risks, are based on best research evidence, and guide practitioners to focus on aspects of client functioning that research, theory, practice experience, and Native wisdom has identified as fundamental to the promotion of children capacities and well-being.

An important point to make about the CASPARS is their capacity to create a common language, to identify significant areas of children functioning, and to coordinate practice across settings. In addition, though the CASPARS provide for agency-level goals, they also do not preclude individualized goals for particular cases. Furthermore, individualized goals are likely to fit within the broad scope of the concepts of the CASPARS.

Some issues are simply part of social services. Holding meaningful conversations with children can be challenging. Service providers may have various reasons for inflating and deflating their assessment of children and the services children are receiving. This, too, is a training issue.

Practitioners were distraught about the demands of paperwork, not only in terms of the sheer amount but also in terms of their redundancy. Before implementing the CASPARS, agency administrators would be fostering more effective use of the CASPARS if they conducted a paperwork audit. There may be ways to streamline paperwork.

Creating data management programs that require a single entry for information that is required on multiple forms would be a great boost to reducing practitioner stress about paperwork.

In summary, the CASPARS have much to recommend them. They point the way to more effective ways to gain balanced views of children and to provide services that promote children's optimal development. Completing the circle so that children in turn can provide resources, modeling, counseling, and guidance to others is a lofty ideal but a worthy one

*Note*: This manual is based largely on the following peer-reviewed articles and book chapter.

Gilgun, Jane F. (2004a). A strengths-based approach to child and family assessment. In Don R. Catheral (Ed.), *Handbook of stress, trauma and the family* (pp. 307-324). New York: Bruner-Routledge. Peer and blind reviewed.

Gilgun, Jane F. (2004b). Qualitative methods and the development of clinical assessment tools. *Qualitative Health Research, 14(7),* 1008-1019.

Gilgun, J.F. (1999a). CASPARS: New tools for assessing client risks and strengths. *Families in Society, 80,* 450-459.
    http://www.cehd.umn.edu/SSW/About_SSW/Faculty_Staff/profiles/Gilgun_publications.asp

Gilgun, Jane F., Susan Keskinen, Danette Jones Marti, & Kay Rice. (1999). Clinical applications of the CASPARS instruments: Boys who act out sexually. *Families in Society, 80,* 629-641.

## References

Bowlby, J. (1973). *Attachment and loss. Vol. II. Separation.* New York: Basic Books.

Baker, M.R. & Steiner, J.R. (1995). Solution-focused social work: Metamessages to students in Higher Education Opportunity Programs. *Social Work, 40,* 225-232).

Beck, B.M. (1997). Clients' right to effective treatment: Readers' responses. *Social Work, 42,* 620.

Berlin, S.B., & Marsh, J.C.. (1993). *Informing practice decisions.* New York: Macmillan.

Bloom, M., Fischer, J. & Orme, J.G. (1999). *Evaluating practice: Guidelines for the accountable professional* (3rd ed.). Boston: Allyn and Bacon.

Boyum, L.A., & Parke, R.D. (1995). The role of family emotional expressiveness in the development of children's social competence. *Journal of Marriage & the Family, 57,* 593-608.

Brendtro, L.K., Brokenleg, M. & Van Bockern, S. (1990). *Reclaiming youth at risk: Our hope for the future.* Bloomington, IN: National Educational Service.

Cassidy, J., & Asher, S.R. (1992). Loneliness and peer relations in young children. *Child Development, 63,* 350-365.

Cicchetti, D. (1987). Developmental psychopathology in infancy: Illustrations from the study of maltreated youngsters. *Journal of Consulting and Clinical Psychology, 55,* 837-845.

Cicchetti, D., Rogosch, F.A., Lynch, M. & Holt, K.D. (1993). Resilience in maltreated children: Processes leading to adaptive outcomes. *Development and Psychopathology, 5,* 629-647.

Compton, B.R., & Galaway, B. (1999). *Social work processes* (6th ed.). Pacific Grove, CA: Brooks/Cole.

Cowger, C.D. (1994). Assessing client strengths: Clinical assessment for client empowerment. *Social Work, 39,* 262-268.

DeJong, P., & Miller, S.D. (1996). How to interview for client strengths. *Social Work, 40,* 729-736.

DeVellis, R.F. (1991). *Scale development: Theory and applications.* Newbury Park, CA: Sage.

Egeland, B., Carlson, E., & Sroufe, L.A. (1993). Resilience as process. *Development and Psychopathology, 5,* 517-528.

Friedrich, W.N., Grambsch, P., Damon, L. Hewitt, S.K. Koverola, C., Lang, R.A., Wolfe, V. & Broughton, D. (1992). Child Sexual Behavior Inventory: Normative and clinical comparisons. *Psychological Assessment, 4,* 303-311.

Erikson, E. (1950/1963). *Childhood and society* (2nd ed.). New York: Norton.

Erickson, M.F., Korfmacher, J., & Egeland, B. (1992). Attachments past and present: Implications for therapeutic intervention with mother-infant dyads. *Development and Psychopathology, 4,* 495-507.

Evidence-Based Medicine Working Group (1992). Evidence-based medicine: A new approach to teaching the practice of medicine. *JAMA (268),* 2420-2425.

Fraiberg, S., Adelson, E., & Shapiro, V. (1975). Ghosts in the nursery: A psychoanalytic approach to the problems of impaired mother-child relationships. *Journal of the American Association of Child Psychiatry, 14,* 387-421.

Fraser, M.W. (1997). (Ed.). *Risk and resilience in childhood.* Washington, D.C.: NASW.

Garmezy, N., & Masten, A.S. (1994). Chronic adversities. In M. Rutter, E. Taylor, & L. Hersov (Eds.), *Child and adolescent psychiatry.* Oxford: Blackwell.

Gil, E., & Johnson, T.C. (1993). *Sexualized children.* Rockville, MD: Launch.

Gilgun, Jane F. (2006). Children and adolescents with problematic sexual behaviors: Lessons from research on resilience. In Robert Longo & Dave Prescott (Eds.), *Current perspectives on working with sexually aggressive youth and youth with sexual behavior problems* (pp. 383-394). Holyoke, MA: Neari Press.

Gilgun, Jane F., & Laura S. Abrams (2005). Gendered adaptations, resilience, and the perpetration of violence. In Michael Ungar (Ed.), *Handbook for working with children and Youth: Pathways to resilience across cultures and context* (pp. 57-70). Toronto: University of Toronto Press

Gilgun, Jane F., Danette Jones, & Kay Rice. (2005). Emotional expressiveness as an indicator of progress in treatment. In Martin C. Calder (Ed.), *Emerging approaches to work with children and young people who sexually abuse* (pp. 231-244). Dorset, England: Russell House.

Gilgun, Jane F. (2005). The four cornerstones of evidence-based practice in social work. *Research on Social Work Practice,* 15(1), 52-61.

Gilgun, Jane F. (2004a). A strengths-based approach to child and family assessment. In Don R. Catheral (Ed.), *Handbook of stress, trauma and the family* (pp. 307-324). New York: Bruner-Routledge.

Gilgun, Jane F. (2004b). Qualitative methods and the development of clinical assessment tools. *Qualitative Health Research,* 14(7), 1008-1019.

Gilgun, Jane F. (2004c). The 4-D: Strengths-based assessments for youth who've experienced adversities. *Journal of Human Behavior in the Social Environment, 10 (4),* 51-73.

Gilgun, J F. (2002). Completing the Circle: American Indian Medicine Wheels and the promotion of resilience in children and youth in care. *Journal of Human Behavior and the Social Environment, 6(2),* 65-84.

Gilgun, J.F. (2002). Social work and the assessment of the potential for violence. In T. N. Tiong, & Dodds, I. (Eds.), *Social work around the world II* (pp. 58-74). Berne, Switzerland: International Federation of Social Workers.

Gilgun, J.F. (2000, June). A comprehensive theory of interpersonal violence. Paper presented at Victimization of Children and Youth: An International Research Conference, Durham, NH, June 25-28.

Gilgun, J.F. (1999a). CASPARS: New tools for assessing client risks and strengths. *Families in Society, 80*, 450-459. Tools available at http://www.cehd.umn.edu/SSW/About_SSW/Faculty_Staff/profiles/Gilgun_publications.asp

Gilgun, J.F. (1999b). Mapping resilience as process among adults maltreated in childhood. In Hamilton I. McCubbin, Elizabeth A. Thompson, Anne I. Thompson, & Jo A. Futrell (Eds.), *The dynamics of resilient families.* (pp. 41-70*).* Thousand Oaks, CA: Sage.

Gilgun, J.F. (1996a). Human development and adversity in ecological perspective: Part 1: A conceptual framework. *Families in Society, 77*, 395-402.

Gilgun, J.F. (1996b). Human development and adversity in ecological perspective, Part 2: Three patterns. *Families in Society, 77*, 459-576.

Gilgun, J.F. (1992). Hypothesis generation in social work research. *Journal of Social Service Research, 15*, 113-135.

Gilgun, J.F. (1991). Resilience and the intergenerational transmission of child sexual abuse. In M. Q. Patton (Ed.), *Family sexual abuse: Frontline research and evaluation* (pp.93-105). Newbury Park, CA: Sage.

Gilgun, J.F. (1990). Factors mediating the effects of childhood maltreatment. In M. Hunter (Ed.), *The sexually abused male: Prevalence, impact, and treatment* (pp. 177-190). Lexington, MA: Lexington Books.

Gilgun, J.F. Klein, C., & Pranis, K. (2000). The significance of resources in models of risk, *Journal of Interpersonal Violence, 14*, 627-646.

Gilgun, J.F., Keskinen, S., Marti, D.J. & Rice, K. (1999). Clinical applications of the CASPARS instruments: Boys who act out sexually. *Families in Society, 80*, 629-641. Tools available at: http://www.cehd.umn.edu/SSW/About_SSW/Faculty_Staff/profiles/Gilgun_publications.asp

Goldstein, H. (1990). Strength or pathology: Ethical and rhetorical contrasts in approaches to practice. *Families in Society, 71*, 267-275.

Gray, S.H. (2002). Evidence-based psychotherapeutics: Presidential Address to the American Academy of Psychoanalysis. *Journal of the American Academy of Psychoanalysis, 30(1)*, 3-16.

Greene, G.J., Jensen, C. & Jones, D.H. (1996). A constructivist perspective on clinical social work practice with ethnically diverse clients. *Social Work, 41*, 172-180.

Halberstadt, A.G., Cassidy, J., Stifter, C.A., Parke, R.D., & Fox, N.A. (1995). Self-expressiveness within the family context: Psychometric support for a new measure. *Psychological Assessment, 7*, 93-103.

Kwang, S. & Cowger, C.D. (1998). Utilizing strengths in assessment. *Families in Society, 79*, 25-31.

Miller, L., Klein, R.G., Piacentini, J., Abikoff, H., Shah, M.R., Samoilov, A., & Guardino, M. (1995). The New York Teacher Rating Scale for Disruptive and Antisocial Behavior. *Journal of the American Academy of Child and Adolescent Psychiatry, 34*, 359-370.

Mahoney, J.L., & Bergman, L.R. (2002). Conceptual and methodological considerations in developmental approach to the study of positive adaptation. *Applied Developmental Psychology, 23*, 195-217.

Masten, A.S. (1994). Resilience in individual development: Successful adaptation despite risk and adversity. In M. C. Wang & E. W. Gordon (Eds.), *Educational resilience in Inner-City America: Challenges and prospects* (pp. 3-23). Hillsdale, NJ: Erlbaum.

Masten, A.S., & Garmezy, N. (1985). Risk, vulnerability, and protective factors in developmental psychopathology. In B. B. Lahey & Alan E. Kazdin (Eds.), *Advances in clinical child psychology (Vol. 8)*,pp. 1-52). New York: Plenum.

Masten, A.S & Wright, M.O. (1998). Cumulative risk and protection models of child maltreatment (1998). *Journal of Aggression, Maltreatment & Trauma, 2(1)*, 7-30

Masten, A.S., Best, K.M. & Garmezy, N. (1991). Resilience and development: Contributions from the study of children who overcome adversity. *Development and Psychopathology, 2*, 425-444.

Miller, S.D., Duncan, B.L., & Hubble, M.A. (1997). *Escape from Babel: Toward a unifying language for psychotherapy practice.* New York: W. W. Norton.

Nunnally, J.C. (1978*). Psychometric theory* (2nd ed.). New York: McGraw-Hill.

Parke, R.D., & Ladd, G.W. (1992). *Family-peer relationships: Modes of linkage.* Hillsdale, N.J.: Erlbaum

Parker, J.G., & Asher, S.R. (1987). Peer relations and later social adjustment: Are low accepted children at risk? *Psychological Bulletin, 102*, 357-359.

Rende, R., & Plomin, R. (1993). Families at risk for psychopathology: Who becomes affected and why? *Development and Psychopathology, 5*, 529-540.

Richters, J.E., & Martinez, P.E. (1993). Violent communities, family choices, and children's chances: An algorithm for improving the odds. *Development and Psychopathology, 5*, 609-627.

Roberts, W., & Strayer, J. (1996). Empathy, emotional expressiveness, and prosocial behavior. *Child Development, 67*, 449-470.

Rutter, M. (1987). Psychosocial resilience and protective mechanisms. *American Journal of Orthopsychiatry, 57*, 316-331.

Sackett, D.L., Straus, S.E., Richardson, W.S., Rosenberg, W., & Haynes, R.B. (2000). *Evidence-based medicine: How to practice and teach EBM* (2nd ed.) Edinburgh: Churchill Livingston.

Salter, A.C. (1988). *Treating child sex offenders and victims.* Newbury Park, CA: Sage.

Saleebey, D. (1996). The strengths perspective in social work practice: Extensions and cautions. *Social Work, 41*, 241-336.

Saleebey, D. (Ed.) (2002). *The strengths perspective in social work practice* (3rd ed). New York: Longman.

Smith, C., & Carlson, B.E. (1997). Stress, coping and resilience in children and youth. *Social Service Review, 71*, 231-256.

Straus, S., & McAlister, F.A. (2000). Evidence-based medicine: A commentary on common criticisms. *CMAJ-JAMC, 163(7)*, 837-841.

Taynor, J., Nelson, R.W., & Daugherty, W.K. (1990). The family intervention scale: Assessing treatment outcome. *Families in Society, 71*, 202-210.

Tracy, E.M., Whittaker, J.K., Pugh, A. Kapp, S.N. & Overstreet, E.J. (1994). Support networks of primary caregivers receiving family preservation services: An exploratory study. *Families in Society, 75*, 481-489.

Van Eys, P.P, & Dodge, K.A. (1999). Closing the gaps: Developmental psychopathology as a training model for clinical child psychology. *Journal of Clinical Child Psychology, 28(4)*, 467-475.

Werner, E.E., & Smith, R.S. (1992). *Overcoming the odds: High risk children from birth to adulthood.* Ithaca, N.Y.: Cornell University Press.

## *Emotional Expressiveness*

|          |          |          | not known/<br>not observed/ |          |          |          |
|----------|----------|----------|-----------------------------|----------|----------|----------|
| high     | low      |          | absent                      | low      | high     |          |
| **3**    | **2**    | **1**    | **0**                       | **1**    | **2**    | **3**    |

| Assets | | | | Risk Factors | | |
|--------|--------|--------|--------|--------------|--------|--------|

1.  Child shows a range of feelings;
only a few, such as happiness, anger
or sadness

| **3** | | **2** | | **1** | | **0** |

1.  Child does not show a range of feelings;
but shows only a few, such as happiness,
anger or sadness

| **1** | | **2** | | **3** |

2. Child puts own feelings into words

| **3** | | **2** | | **1** | | **0** |

2.  Child does not put own feelings into words

| **1** | | **2** | | **3** |

3.  Child's expression of feelings
is appropriate to situations

| **3** | | **2** | | **1** | | **0** |

3.  Child's expression of feelings
is not appropriate to situations

| **1** | | **2** | | **3** |

4. Child's feelings and reactions
are linked to the events that precipitated them

| **3** | | **2** | | **1** | | **0** |

4.  Child's feelings and reactions are not linked
to the events that precipitated them

| **1** | | **2** | | **3** |

5.  Child can identify a wide range of feelings
in others

| **3** | | **2** | | **1** | | **0** |

5.  Child cannot identify feelings in others

| **1** | | **2** | | **3** |

6.  Child sympathizes with other people's

| **3** | | **2** | | **1** | | **0** |

6.  Child does not sympathize with other feelings
people's feelings

| **1** | | **2** | | **3** |

7.  Child appears to respect the feelings
of others; does not mock, tease, or use others

| **3** | | **2** | | **1** | | **0** |

7. Child does not appear to have respect
for the feelings of others; mocks,
teases, and uses others

| **1** | | **2** | | **3** |

8.  Child has person in family and/or
community who facilitates appropriate
expression of feelings

| **3** | | **2** | | **1** | | **0** |

8.  Child has few or no persons in family
or community who facilitates appropriate
expression of feelings

| **1** | | **2** | | **3** |

9.  Child's moods are fairly even;
rarely has mood swings

| **3** | | **2** | | **1** | | **0** |

9.  Child's moods are not even; has a pattern
has a pattern of mood swings

| **1** | | **2** | | **3** |

10. Child shares emotionally-laden events with others, both positive and hurtful events

    **3**        **2**        **1**

10. Child does not share emotionally-laden events with others

    **1**        **2**        **3**

          **0**

11. Child engages emotionally with others

    **3**        **2**        **1**

11. Child does not engage emotionally with others

    **1**        **2**        **3**

          **0**

12. Child is sensitive to others

    **3**        **2**        **1**

12. Child is not sensitive to others

    **1**        **2**        **3**

          **0**

13. Child is not withdrawn

    **3**        **2**        **1**

13. Child is withdrawn

    **1**        **2**        **3**

          **0**

14. Child's emotional responses match demands of the situation

    **3**        **2**        **1**

14. Child's emotionally responses do not match demands of the situation; child over-reacts or under-reacts

    **1**        **2**        **3**

          **0**

15. Child recognizes when her/his emotional responses are not appropriate

    **3**        **2**        **1**

15. Child does not recognized when emotional responses are not appropriate

    **1**        **2**        **3**

          **0**

16. Child apologizes for inappropriate expressions of feelings

    **3**        **2**        **1**

16. Child does not apologize for inappropriate expressions of feelings

    **1**        **2**        **3**

          **0**

4/3/96

# *Family's and Child's Embeddedness in Community*

|  | | | not known/<br>not observed/ | | |
|---|---|---|---|---|---|
| **high** | **low** | **absent** | **low** | **high** |
| **3** | **2** | **1** | **0** | **1** | **2** | **3** |

| **Assets** | **Risk Factors** |
|---|---|

1. Family members have pleasant social relationships with extended family

    **3**        **2**        **1**        **0**

1. Family members do not have pleasant social relationships with extended family

    **1**        **2**        **3**

2. Family members have pleasant social relationships with friends & neighbors

    **3**        **2**        **1**        **0**

2. Family members do not have pleasant social relationships with friends & neighbors

    **1**        **2**        **3**

3. Family members have family or friends with whom they share resources

    **3**        **2**        **1**        **0**

3. Family members do not have family or friends with whom they share resources

    **1**        **2**        **3**

4. Family members have close friends with whom they share feelings and problems

    **3**        **2**        **1**        **0**

4. Family members do not have close friends with whom they share

    **1**        **2**        **3**

5. Family members enjoy their work; their work has meaning to them

    **3**        **2**        **1**        **0**

5. Family members do not enjoy their work; their work has little if any to meaning to them

    **1**        **2**        **3**

6. Family members have pleasant relationships with persons at schools, religious organizations,, libraries, and stores

    **3**        **2**        **1**        **0**

6. Family members do not have pleasant relationships with persons at schools, religious organization, libraries, and stores

    **1**        **2**        **3**

7. Family members are involved in positive community activities, such as PTA or helping at religious organizations

    **3**        **2**        **1**        **0**

7. Family members are not involved in positive community activities, such as PTA or helping at religious organizations

    **1**        **2**        **3**

8. Family members feel a sense of belonging in the neighborhood and/or larger community

    **3**        **2**        **1**        **0**

8. Families members do not feel a sense of belonging in neighborhood and/or larger community, but experience prejudice, discrimination, and shunning

    **1**        **2**        **3**

9. Family is financially secure

    **3**        **2**        **1**        **0**

9. Family is not financially secure

    **1**        **2**        **3**

10. Neighborhood has resources for children: playgrounds, recreation programs, libraries

   **3**          **2**          **1**          **0**

10. Neighborhood does not have resources for children

   **1**          **2**          **3**

11. Child witnesses adults and others in the neighborhood as living within the law and exhibiting conventional social behaviors

   **3**          **2**          **1**          **0**

11. Child witnesses adults and others in the neighborhood as not living within the law and not exhibiting conventional behaviors but as doing such things as dealing and using drugs or alcohol, and/or being violent through such acts as beatings, sexual assault

   **1**          **2**          **3**

12. The interactions of child with others in the neighborhood are generally civil, not characterized by verbal and/or physical aggression and/or intimidation

   **3**          **2**          **1**          **0**

12. The interaction of child with others in the neighborhood generally are not civil, but are characterized by verbal and/or physical aggression and/or intimidation

   **1**          **2**          **3**

13. Child reports school and/or community experiences where adults and/or older children give positive reinforcement

   **3**          **2**          **1**          **0**

13. Child does not report school or community experiences that give positive reinforcement

   **1**          **2**          **3**

4/9/96

## *Peer Relationships*

| | high | | low | not known/ not observed/ absent | low | | high | |
|---|---|---|---|---|---|---|---|---|
| **3** | | **2** | **1** | **0** | **1** | **2** | **3** | |

| Assets | Risk Factors |
|---|---|

**Assets**

1. Child spends time with same-age children

3     2     1     0

2. Child's seeks relationships with other children who are about the same age

3     2     1     0

3. Other children seek child out to spend time with child

3     2     1     0

4. Child spends time with other children who do not get in trouble

3     2     1     0

5. Child can do things most kids do, such as ride bikes, play sports, or do well in games at home, school and/or neighborhood

3     2     1     0

6. Child has interests similar to those of age peers

3     2     1     0

7. Child has maintained a relationship over time with another child who is about the same age

3     2     1     0

8. Child has a sense of belonging within peer groups, through Scouts, sports, or other group activities

3     2     1     0

**Risk Factors**

1. Child does not spend time with same-age children

1     2     3

2. Child does not seek relationships with other children who are about the same age

1     2     3

3. Other children do not seek child out to spend time with child

1     2     3

4. Child spends time with other children who get in trouble

1     2     3

5. Child cannot do things most kids do, such as ride bikes, play sports, or do well in games at home, school, and/or neighborhood

1     2     3

6. Child does not have interests similar to age peers

1     2     3

7. Child has not maintained a relationship over time with another child who is about the same age

1     2     3

8. Child does not have a sense of belonging within peer groups, through Scouts, sports, or other group activities

1     2     3

9. Child reports school or community
experiences where adults and/or older children
give positive reinforcement to child

**3**         **2**         **1**         **0**

9. Child does not report school or community
experiences that give positive reinforcement
to the child

**1**         **2**         **3**

10. Child reports school and/or community
experiences where adults and/or older children
give positive reinforcement to peers

**3**         **2**         **1**         **0**

10. Child does not report school or community
experiences that give positive reinforcement
to peers

**1**         **2**         **3**

11. Child enters into new activities and situations
with a sense of adventure and confidence

**3**         **2**         **1**         **0**

11. Child does not enter into new situations
and activities with a sense of adventure
and confidence but with a sense of dread
and fear of failure

**1**         **2**         **3**

12. Child does at least as well as peers
in academic subjects at school

**3**         **2**         **1**         **0**

12. Child does not do at least as well as peers
in academic subjects in school

**1**         **2**         **3**

13. Child does at least one thing well,
such as caring for an animal, having a hobby,
or a sport

**3**         **2**         **1**         **0**

13. Child does not do at least one thing well

**1**         **2**         **3**

14. Child and peers talk out their differences

**3**         **2**         **1**         **0**

14. Child and peers do not talk out their differences

**1**         **2**         **3**

15. The interactions of child with peers
are generally civil, characterized by little
verbal and/or physical aggression
withdrawal, silent treatments,
and abandonments, and/or threats
of abandonments

**3**         **2**         **1**         **0**

15. The interactions of child with peers
are not generally civil, but are
characterized by verbal and/or physical
aggression, withdrawal, silent treatments,
and abandonments and/threats
of abandonments

**1**         **2**         **3**

16. The child stands up for her/himself when
peers behave disrespectfully toward the child

**3**         **2**         **1**         **0**

16. The child does not stand up for her/himself
when peers behave disrespectfully
toward the child

**1**         **2**         **3**

17. Other children are respectful, physically,
sexually, and/or emotionally

**3**         **2**         **1**         **0**

17. Other children are not respectful
but tease, are physically, sexually
aggressive, and/or emotionally cruel

**1**         **2**         **3**

18.  Child has flexible ideas about how boys and girls are "supposed" to act

    **3**        **2**        **1**

18.  Child has does not have flexible ideas about how boys and girls are "supposed" to act; child is inflexible

    **0**        **1**        **2**        **3**

4/9/96

# *Relationships in Family of Origin*

| | | | not known/ not observed/ absent | | | |
|---|---|---|---|---|---|---|
| high | | low | | low | | high |
| **3** | **2** | **1** | **0** | **1** | **2** | **3** |

| Assets | | | | Risk Factors | | |

1.  Parental figures talk out their differences

| **3** | **2** | **1** | **0** | **1** | **2** | **3** |

1.  Parental figures do not talk out their differences

2.  Parental figures manage their problems each has an equal voice

| **3** | **2** | **1** | **0** | **1** | **2** | **3** |

2.  Parents figures do not manage their equitably; problems equitably; each does not have an equal voice

3.  The interactions of parental figures with each other are generally civil, characterized verbal and/or physical aggression and/or intimidation

| **3** | **2** | **1** | **0** | **1** | **2** | **3** |

3.  The interactions of parental figures with each other are not generally civil, but are by little characterized by verbal and/or physical aggression, withdrawal, silent treatments, and abandonments and/or threats of abandonment

4.  Parental figures sympathize with child's problems

| **3** | **2** | **1** | **0** | **1** | **2** | **3** |

4.  Parental figures do not sympathize with child's problems

5.  Child and parental figures talk out their differences

| **3** | **2** | **1** | **0** | **1** | **2** | **3** |

5.  Child and parental figures do not talk out their differences

6.  The interactions of parental figures with child are generally civil, characterized by little verbal and/or physical intimidation aggression, withdrawal, silent treatments abandonments, and/or threats of abandonment

| **3** | **2** | **1** | **0** | **1** | **2** | **3** |

6.  The interactions of parental figures with child are not generally civil, but are characterized by verbal and/or physical intimidation, and/or aggression, withdrawal, silent treatments, abandonments, and/or threats of abandonments

7.  Child and siblings talk out their differences

| **3** | **2** | **1** | **0** | **1** | **2** | **3** |

7.  Child and siblings do not talk out their differences

8. The interactions of child with siblings are generally civil, characterized by little verbal and/or physical aggression, withdrawal, silent treatments, and abandonments and/or threats of abandonment

   **3**         **2**         **1**         **0**

8. The interactions of child with siblings are not generally civil, but are characterized by verbal and/or physical aggression, withdrawal, silent treatments, and abandonments and/or threats of abandonment

   **1**         **2**         **3**

9. Child can confide in one adult or older sibling in the nuclear family

   **3**         **2**         **1**         **0**

9. Child cannot confide in one adult or older sibling in the nuclear family

   **1**         **2**         **3**

10. At least one adult or older sibling the nuclear family is sensitive to the child's feelings

   **3**         **2**         **1**         **0**

10. No adult or older sibling in the family in in the nuclear family is sensitive to the child's feelings

   **1**         **2**         **3**

11. At least one adult or older sibling the nuclear family responds calmly to child's feelings; they do not over-react or under-react

   **3**         **2**         **1**         **0**

11. No adult or older sibling in the nuclear family responds calmly to child's feelings; they over-react and/or under-react

   **1**         **2**         **3**

12. At least one adult or older sibling in the nuclear family is interested in the child's activities

   **3**         **2**         **1**         **0**

12. No adult or older sibling in the nuclear family is interested in the child's activities

   **1**         **2**         **3**

13. At least one adult or older sibling in the nuclear family communicates with the child in ways that are honest, direct, and kind

   **3**         **2**         **1**         **0**

13. No adult or older sibling in the nuclear family communicates with the child in ways that are honest, direct, and kind

   **1**         **2**         **3**

14. Discipline is authoritative

   **3**         **2**         **1**         **0**

14. Discipline is not authoritative

   **1**         **2**         **3**

15. Discipline is consistent

   **3**         **2**         **1**         **0**

15. Discipline is not consistent

   **1**         **2**         **3**

16. Discipline is not authoritarian

   **3**         **2**         **1**         **0**

16. Discipline is authoritarian

   **1**         **2**         **3**

17. Discipline is not laissez-faire

   **3**         **2**         **1**         **0**

17. Discipline is laissez-faire

   **1**         **2**         **3**

18. Parental figures communicate clear expectations

   **3**         **2**         **1**         **0**

18. Parental figures do not communicate clear expectations

   **1**         **2**         **3**

19. Parental figures recognize children's successes

   **3**         **2**         **1**         **0**

19. Parental figures do not acknowledge children's successes

**1**         **2**         **3**

20. Child's household responsibilities are age-appropriate

   **3**         **2**         **1**         **0**

20. Child's household chores are not age-appropriate

**1**         **2**         **3**

21. Siblings are respectful, physically, sexually, and/or emotionally

   **3**         **2**         **1**         **0**

21. Siblings are not respectful, physically, sexually, emotionally

**1**         **2**         **3**

22. When siblings are disrespectful or cruel, child responds assertively

   **3**         **2**         **1**         **0**

22. When siblings are disrespectful or cruel, child responds aggressively, indirectly aggressively, or internalizes the hurt and/or rage; may fantasize about revenge or feel entitled to use others to feel better

**1**         **2**         **3**

23. Adults and older siblings in the nuclear family respect child's physical boundaries; they do not, for example, use child's things without permission and/or disrespect child's sense of personal private space

   **3**         **2**         **1**         **0**

23. Adults and older siblings in the nuclear family do not respect the child's physical boundaries; they use child's things without child's permission and/or they disrespect child's sense of personal private space

**1**         **2**         **3**

24. Parents and older siblings respect emotional boundaries and do not seek and/or emotional support from the child

   **3**         **2**         **1**         **0**

24. Parents and older siblings do not respect emotional boundaries and seek advice and/or emotional support from the child

**1**         **2**         **3**

25. Family members have a variety of emotional outlets, such as talking things out, exercising, and entertainment

   **3**         **2**         **1**         **0**

25. Family members have few emotional outlets, rarely if ever talking things out or dealing constructively with emotions

**1**         **2**         **3**

26. Family members discuss losses of other family members through death, separations, hospitalizations

   **3**         **2**         **1**         **0**

26. Family members do not discuss their losses

**1**         **2**         **3**

27. Family members do not abuse chemicals and/or are not actively chemically dependent

   **3**         **2**         **1**         **0**

27. Family members abuse chemicals and/or are actively chemically dependent

**1**         **2**         **3**

28. Family members have not served time in jail or prison

   **3**         **2**         **1**         **0**

28. Family members have served time in jail or prison

**1**         **2**         **3**

29. There is no history of psychiatric
illness in the nuclear family

|  |  |  |  |
|---|---|---|---|
| **3** | **2** | **1** | **0** |

29. There is a history of psychiatric
illness in the nuclear family

|  |  |  |
|---|---|---|
| **1** | **2** | **3** |

30. Parental figures are able to manage
household expenses with the income they receive

|  |  |  |  |  |  |  |
|---|---|---|---|---|---|---|
| **3** | **2** | **1** | **0** | **1** | **2** | **3** |

30. Parental figures are not able to handle
household expenses with the income they
receive

4/9/96

## *Sexuality*

|  high |  | low | not known/<br>not observed/<br>absent |  | low |  | high |  |
|---|---|---|---|---|---|---|---|---|
| 3 | 2 | 1 | 0 | | 1 | 2 | 3 | |
| **Assets** | | | | | | **Risk Factors** | | |

1  Parents set limits on child's masturbation, exposing of genitals, and touching the sexual body parts of others

Parents do not set limits on child's masturbation, exposing of genitals, and touching the sexual body parts of others.

| 3 | 2 | 1 | 0 | 1 | 2 | 3 |
|---|---|---|---|---|---|---|

2. Child stops sexually inappropriate behaviors when parents set limits

Child does not stop sexually inappropriate behaviors when parents s

| 3 | 2 | 1 | 0 | 1 | 2 | 3 |
|---|---|---|---|---|---|---|

3.  Child never or occasionally masturbates while looking at nude or semi-nude pictures in newspapers, magazines, and catalogues, such as lingerie ads

Child frequently or often masturbates by looking at nude or semi-nude pictures in magazines, newspapers, and catalogues, such as lingerie ads

| 3 | 2 | 1 | 0 | 1 | 2 | 3 |
|---|---|---|---|---|---|---|

4.  Child respects sexual boundaries

Child does not respect sexual boundaries

| 3 | 2 | 1 | 0 | 1 | 2 | 3 |
|---|---|---|---|---|---|---|

5.  Child does not have a pattern attributing sexual behaviors to dolls and other toys

Child has a pattern of attributing sexual behaviors to dolls and other toys

| 3 | 2 | 1 | 0 | 1 | 2 | 3 |
|---|---|---|---|---|---|---|

6. Child respects the sexual boundaries of animals

Child does not respect the sexual boundaries of animals

| 3 | 2 | 1 | 0 | 1 | 2 | 3 |
|---|---|---|---|---|---|---|

7.  Child occasionally or never engages; in sex play, defined as mutual and with children of similar age

Child engages in non-mutual sexual behaviors, defined as coercive and/or manipulative

| 3 | 2 | 1 | 0 | 1 | 2 | 3 |
|---|---|---|---|---|---|---|

8.  Child has a sense of when to talk about sexual things

Child does not have a good sense of when to talk about sexual things

| 3 | 2 | 1 | 0 | 1 | 2 | 3 |
|---|---|---|---|---|---|---|

11.  Parents have provided child with information about sexuality that is age appropriate

Parents have not provided child with information about sexuality that is age appropriate

| 3 | 2 | 1 | 0 | 1 | 2 | 3 |
|---|---|---|---|---|---|---|

12. Parents respect the sexual boundaries others, keeping their own sexual behaviors private

| | | | |
|---|---|---|---|
| 3 | 2 | 1 | 0 |

Parents do not respect the sexual boundaries of others; they do not keep their sexual behaviors private

| | | |
|---|---|---|
| 1 | 2 | 3 |

13. Other persons in child's environments keep their own sexual behavior private

| | | | |
|---|---|---|---|
| 3 | 2 | 1 | 0 |

Other persons in child's environment do not keep their own sexual behaviors private

| | | |
|---|---|---|
| 1 | 2 | 3 |

14. The sexual behaviors child has witnessed in the past are appropriate, such as affectionate kissing, affectionate hugging, and affectionate talks and looks

| | | | |
|---|---|---|---|
| 3 | 2 | 1 | 0 |

The sexual behaviors that child has witnessed in the past are not appropriate, and include intercourse, forced/coerced sexual contact such as rape and child sexual abuse, and genital touching even if consensual

| | | |
|---|---|---|
| 1 | 2 | 3 |

15. The sexual behaviors child currently is witnessing are appropriate, such as affectionate kissing, affectionate hugging, and affectionate talks and looks

| | | | |
|---|---|---|---|
| 3 | 2 | 1 | 0 |

The sexual behaviors the child currently is witnessing are not appropriate and include forced/coerced sexual contact such as rape and child sexual abuse, genital touching even if consensual

| | | |
|---|---|---|
| 1 | 2 | 3 |

16. The sexual talk in the family to which the child is exposed is respectful, of the child and of others

| | | | |
|---|---|---|---|
| 3 | 2 | 1 | 0 |

The sexual talk in the family to which the child is exposed is not respectful of the child or others, but is objectifying and denigrating

| | | |
|---|---|---|
| 1 | 2 | 3 |

17. In general, the environments to which the child is exposed is respectful of the child's sexuality and the sexuality of others

| | | | |
|---|---|---|---|
| 3 | 2 | 1 | 0 |

In general, the environments to which child is exposed is not respectful of the child's sexuality and the sexuality of others

| | | |
|---|---|---|
| 1 | 2 | 3 |

18. Materials with sexual content to which child is exposed are age appropriate; these materials include books, videos, computer games, cable tv, and internet information

| | | | |
|---|---|---|---|
| 3 | 2 | 1 | 0 |

Materials with sexual content to which child is exposed is not age appropriate; these materials include books, videos, computer games, cable tv, and information on the internet that depicts sadism, violence, and abuse

| | | |
|---|---|---|
| 1 | 2 | 3 |

19. Overall, child is appropriate sexually

| | | | |
|---|---|---|---|
| 3 | 2 | 1 | 0 |

Overall, child is not appropriate sexually

| | | |
|---|---|---|
| 1 | 2 | 3 |

4/3/96

First published in the United States of America in 1998

Gilgun, Jane.
The CASPARS: Clinical Instruments for Client Risks & Strengths


ISBN-13: 978-1479222407

ISBN-10: 1479222402

Createspace


1. Child development  2. Clinical assessment 3. Parenting 4. Social services
5. children & families 6. Childhood sexuality 7. Resilience.

Visit Amazon Kindle, Google Books, iBooks, & other Internet booksellers
to discover other books, articles, and children's stories by Jane Gilgun
that you may enjoy.